CULTIVATING STRENGTH & VITALITY

By

Sri Mata Amritanandamayi Devi

Delivered on December 1st 2009

Address at the Inauguration of the
Vivekananda International Foundation
in New Delhi

Translated by
Swami Amritaswarupananda Puri

Mata Amritanandamayi Mission Trust
Amritapuri, Kerala, India

CULTIVATING STRENGTH & VITALITY
An Address by Sri Mata Amritanandamayi Devi
Translated by Swami Amritaswarupananda Puri

Published by
  Mata Amritanandamayi Mission Trust
  Amritapuri P.O., Kollam Dt.
  Kerala 690 525, India
  Email: info@theammashop.org
  Website: www.amritapuri.org

Copyright © 2010 Mata Amritanandamayi Mission Trust

All rights reserved. No part of this publication may be stored in a retrieval system, transmitted, reproduced, transcribed or translated into any language, in any form, by any means without the prior agreement and written permission of the publisher.

First edition: January 2010, 3000 copies
Second edition: June 2010, 2500 copies
Third edition: June 2011, 2000 copies
Fourth edition: June 2012, 1000 copies

(l-r) Sri. Ajit Kumar Doval, Director of Vivekananda International Foundation; Honourable M.N. Venkatacheliah, former Chief Justice of India; Sri Mata Amritanandamayi Devi; P. Parameshwaran, President of Vivekananda Kendra

FOREWORD

This short speech was Amma's address for the inauguration of the Vivekananda International Foundation in Chanakyapuri, New Delhi on December 1, 2009. In fact, Amma's words do not need a foreword; they are simple, lucid and self-explanatory. The speech was delivered to an august assembly of intellectuals and high officials of Delhi. It is not long, yet it contains the essence of spirituality.

In the address, Amma touches on a wide range of topics, including the means of creating interreligious harmony, the proper role of education in society and the importance of taking pride in one's motherland and national heritage. Her main focus, however, is on the youth—their needs and the role adults should play in helping them attain their full potential.

Each subject is dealt with concisely, with an insight that penetrates to the core of the issue. And as the words come from such a unique spiritual master, it goes without saying that the speech is profound, lively and spiritually vibrant.

Speaking about the remarkable personality

that was Swami Vivekananda, Amma said, "Swami Vivekananda—the name in itself has a special power and allure. Its bearer was such a radiant being that just by hearing the name we automatically feel awakened and energized. He was a great sannyasi who revolutionized and transformed society, a perfect jnani, the epitome of devotion to the guru, an elevated karma yogi and a brilliant orator." Amma described Vivekananda's vision of spirituality as "a way of living to be performed in this world, while interacting with all types of people and facing all circumstances and challenges with courage and composure."

Offering beautiful anecdotes and stories, Amma explained how mahatmas are living examples of spiritual truths. The scriptures and scriptural dictums come alive only through the life and teachings of a Self-realized master. The sadguru [true spiritual master] is an embodiment of all divine qualities. As Amma said, "Their lives are the greatest examples for society to imbibe. This is what maintains harmony in society."

Stressing the importance of awakening spiritual strength, Amma said, "When God's

Foreword

power shines through us, it manifests as truth, auspiciousness and beauty. When God manifests through the intellect, truth shines forth. When God manifests through actions, it does so as goodness and auspiciousness. And when God manifests through the heart, beauty is the result. When truth, auspiciousness and beauty blend in our life, true strength awakens."

Amma understands better than anyone just how essential it is that our youth receive education in spiritual matters. Amma knows that the younger generation possesses tremendous energy. If that energy is properly channelled, our youth can perform wonders. If they change, the world will change. Across the globe, I have witnessed thousands of young men and women transform due to Amma's presence in their lives—their attitudes, their perspective about life. Without doubt, this is creating a constructive change in society. The youth who come in contact with Amma become more aware about their dharma [duty] towards themselves and society. They become eager to selflessly serve society, the poor and needy, and to protect the environment. However, speaking about the condition of today's youth in general, Amma expresses concern. "Today, the phase of human life known as 'youth' is disappearing," she said in Delhi. "We jump straight from childhood into old age. In fact, youth is the bindu—the centre-point of life. It is a time when we are neither child nor adult. It is a time for living in the moment as well as the ideal stage for training the mind. But is the present generation properly making use of this period?"

Amma said that today's youth are not satisfied with mere words and information. They need inspiring examples, role models. Furthermore, even though the texts of Sanatana Dharma are treasure houses of immense knowledge, they need to be presented in a manner that helps modern youth to appreciate them. For this to happen, the older generation needs to properly understand the younger generation and approach them with an attitude of humility and love. Amma said this approach needs to be one of 'dialogue'—patiently listening to them and imparting the knowledge with maturity and compassion.

Amma also said that we need to re-examine the methodology and language used when

Foreword

conducting interreligious discussions. Expressing concern regarding the current tendency of religious leaders to twist religious truths to serve their selfish purposes, Amma said, "Religion and spirituality are keys meant to open our hearts, enabling us to view everyone with compassion. ... Due to our of lack of discrimination, the very keys meant to open our hearts are locking them shut."

Amma also pointed out certain ways in which our modern education system is misleading society. "The foundation of all positive change is true education," Amma said. She described true education as the secret mantra for obtaining success in life and the solution to all problems. However, Amma said, "Our education system has been reduced to a tool for obtaining material success."

Today's world, particularly the younger generation, only believes in human effort. This only serves to inflate the ego. What we need today is egoless, compassionate leadership. Amma always emphasizes the necessity of divine grace for attaining success, regardless of the field. Amma believes it is crucial that modern youth understand the importance of the grace factor, which is beyond comprehension or logic. Amma said, "We should eliminate the egoistic notion that our life will become fruitful through human effort alone. We should bow down. Only then will the power supporting the cosmos flow into us."

Amma concluded the speech by highlighting the significance of love for one's own country. She extolled Swami Vivekananda as a strong patriot who loved India and its rich culture. "Our heritage is incomparable," Amma said. "We should adopt the good from other countries while remaining firmly rooted in love for our own country and spiritual culture."

Reflecting on Amma's words of wisdom, the Honourable M.N. Venkatachaliah, former Chief Justice of India and renowned scholar, said, "Today we had this dose of amrita [ambrosia] from Amma. She told us what adds flavour to life, and her interpretation of Vivekananda was perhaps the most inspirational and accurate. And her understanding and presentation was so remarkable that I think some of us who felt gloomy now feel that as yet that there is something that is good for the world. Someone once said, 'As long as there are

Foreword

birds, flowers and children, everything will be all right with the world.' But I say, 'As long as there are birds, flowers and children and Mata Amritanandamayi, everything will be all right with the world.'"

Sri. Ajit Kumar Doval, the Director of Vivekananda International Foundation, referred to Amma as "spirituality incarnate," saying, "Amma's abiding love for humanity and her all-pervading energy are in line with the great tradition of our spiritual leaders, who from time to time lead humanity and the destiny of this nation, providing a sense of continuity to our civilization—that civilization that constitutes the bedrock of our nationalism, of our identity, of our nation and its people."

Swami Amritaswarupananda
Vice-Chairman
Mata Amritanandamayi Math

Amma delivering her address in New Delhi at the Vivekananda International Foundation.

CULTIVATING STRENGTH & VITALITY

By Sri Mata Amritanandamayi Devi

Delivered on December 1st 2009

Address for the Inauguration of the Vivekananda International Foundation in New Delhi

Amma is delighted that such an institution has arisen in the name of Swami Vivekananda for the sake of interreligious harmony and unity, and for sharing the values of Sanatana Dharma[1] with the rest of the world. *Swami Vivekananda*—the name in itself has a special power and allure. Its bearer was such a radiant being that just by hearing the name, we automatically feel awakened and energized.

---

[1] Literally, 'eternal universal laws,' the original name for Hinduism; it is considered eternal because its core principles are universal, holding true regardless of time or place.

He was a great *sannyasi*[2] who revolutionized and transformed society, a perfect *jnani*[3], the epitome of devotion to the *guru*[4], an elevated *karma yogi*[5] and a brilliant orator. All in all, Swami Vivekananda was an extremely rare individual—a divine flower that, brought to blossom under the spiritual effulgence of Sri Ramakrishna Deva, went on to spread beautiful fragrance throughout the world.

For Swami Vivekananda, spirituality was not penance to be performed with closed eyes in some faraway forest or cave, but a way of living to be performed in this world, while interacting with all types of people and facing all circumstances and challenges with courage and composure. He firmly believed that spirituality is the foundation of life and the source of true strength and intelligence.

---

[2] One who has renounced worldly life for spiritual liberation.
[3] Literally, 'a knower'—one who has realized the transcendental truth.
[4] A spiritual teacher.
[5] One who performs all actions as an offering to God and, in turn, equanimously accepts all of life's situations, positive and negative alike, as God's sacred gift.

Compassion and concern for one's fellow beings was the very core of Swami Vivekananda's concept of spirituality. He proclaimed that he would not believe in a God or religion that could not wipe the widow's tears or bring a piece of bread to the orphan's mouth. Stressing compassion and service to the world, he added a new dimension to the Indian tradition of *sannyasa*.

The lives of *mahatmas*[6] are their message. Their lives are the greatest examples for society to imbibe. This is what maintains harmony in society. The fact that India's family bonds and social values have remained vibrant is primarily due to the influence and inspiration of the lives of mahatmas. They didn't merely teach dictums such as "Always speak truth. Always follow righteousness"[7] and "May your mother, father, teachers and guests be God to you,"[8] but lived them. Values took root in society not from the

---

[6] Literally, 'great souls'; Amma uses the word to specifically indicate those who have attained Self-realization.
[7] *satyaṁ vada | dharmaṁ cara |* [Taittiriya Upanishad, 1.11.1]
[8] *mātṛdevo bhava | pitṛdevo bhava | ācārya-devo bhava | atithidevo bhava |* [Taittiriya Upanishad, 1.11.12]

examples set by kings and political leaders but from those set by mahatmas. In fact, mahatmas were the ones who provided the guidance and examples for the rulers. The foundation of all values is spirituality. If we lose our values, our life becomes like a satellite that has broken free from the earth's gravitational pull.

Mahatmas are not mere individuals. They are visible forms of the ultimate truth. Selfishness has been eradicated within them. Just as a magnet attracts iron filings, mahatmas attract the entire world. Because they perform actions without selfishness or attachment, everything they do transforms society and the world at large.

A group of young men once approached a sannyasi and asked, "What is sannyasa?" At the time, the sannyasi was carrying a bundle of possessions on his back. He immediately dropped the bundle and continued walking. Unable to understand the meaning of the mahatma's action, the young men caught up with him and again asked, "What is sannyasa?"

The mahatma replied, "Didn't you see me

drop the bundle? First of all sannyasa is renunciation of 'I' and 'mine.'"

Curious to know more, the young men asked, "After giving up 'I' and 'mine,' what is the next step?"

The mahatma walked back, picked the bundle up, and again placed it on his back. He then continued walking. Confused, the young men asked him, "What does that mean?"

The sannyasi smiled and replied, "Didn't you see me putting on the bundle again? After giving up 'I' and 'mine,' one must shoulder the burden of the world. Seeing the sorrows and difficulties of others as one's own, one should love and serve them. That is what real sannyasa is."

However this load will not weigh him down because where there is love, there is no burden. Taking care of a child may be a difficult task for a babysitter, but for the child's mother it is a joyful experience. Where there is love, there is no burden.

That said, in order to serve the world selflessly, one has to first become strong.

Swami Vivekananda professed that only through awakening the inner power can we attain true transformation and find permanent solutions to the problems facing society.

Strength is the most important quality for an individual or a country. When we realize that strength resides within, true strength awakens. *Satyam, shivam, sundaram*—truth[9], auspiciousness and beauty—are not qualities of God, they are our experience, how we perceive God. They are, in fact, limits that our mind projects upon God. In reality, God is beyond all qualities—infinite. When God's power shines through us, it manifests as truth, auspiciousness and beauty. When God manifests through the intellect, truth shines forth. When God manifests through actions, it does so as goodness and auspiciousness. And when God manifests through the heart, beauty is the result. When

---

[9] In the context of this paragraph, *satyaṁ*–truth–does not indicate the ultimate reality but qualities such as honesty, integrity and straightforwardness. As Amma says, the ultimate reality of God, as well as the individual and the universe, is beyond all qualities; it is pure consciousness.

truth, auspiciousness and beauty blend in our life, true strength awakens.[10]

What is needed in India[11] is strength, vitality and vigour. If our youth arise and act, they have the strength and dynamism to generate a huge transformation in society.

As Swami Vivekananda once said, "[The] supreme value of youth period is incalculable and indescribable. Youth life is the most precious life. Youth is the best time. The way in which you utilize this period will decide the nature of coming years that lie ahead of you. Your happiness, your success, your honour and your good name all depend upon the way in which you live now, in this present period. Remember this. This wonderful period of the first state of your life is related to you as the soft wet clay in the hands of the potter. Skilfully

---

[10] Consciousness enlivens creation; it is the substratum of the universe. When the mind is purified of likes and dislikes, the enlivened personality expresses divine qualities such as truthfulness, goodness and beauty.

[11] As Amma delivered her address in New Delhi, Amma specifically mentioned 'India' here. However, these qualities are needed in all nations.

the potter gives it the right and correct shapes and forms, which he intends to give. Even so, you can wisely mould your life, your character, your physical health and strength, in short your entire nature in any way in which you make up your mind to do. And you must do this now."

Today, the phase of human life known as "youth" is disappearing. We jump straight from childhood into old age. In fact, youth is the *bindu*—the centre-point of life. It is a time when we are neither child nor adult. It is a time for living in the moment as well as the ideal stage for training the mind. But is the present generation properly making use of this period?

Once, a lady was walking through a park when she saw an old man sitting on a bench, smiling to himself. The lady approached him and said, "You look so happy! What's the secret behind your long and happy life?"

The old man replied, "Well, as soon I get out of bed, I straight off drink two whole bottles of whiskey. Then I smoke a pack of cigarettes. For lunch I eat fried chicken and steak to my heart's content. I spend the rest of the day listening to heavy-metal and rap music. I snack on chips, sweets and other junk food throughout the day. On top of that, I usually smoke ganja four or five times a week. And exercise? I never even think about it!"

The lady was shocked. "Amazing!" she said. "I've never heard of anyone with your kind of lifestyle living to such a ripe old age. By the way, how old are you?"

"Twenty-six," replied the man.

This is how many are wasting their precious youth. What is the reason for this? In childhood, they are not receiving proper discipline from their parents. The whole emphasis is on money and study. These are needed, but we need to take care to instil values in our children as well. Even if a person buys the most expensive car and fills it with the highest grade petrol, a battery is still needed in order to start the engine. Similarly, to drive the vehicle of life, we need values and virtues.

How can young people develop spiritual values and good qualities? How can we lead them on the proper path? How can we channel

the strength of youth to facilitate the growth of society, the country and the world? To achieve this, we have to train our youth to develop their character and unfold as human beings. To do this, we first need to properly understand them. We need to go down to their level. Swami Vivekananda worked stressing these points.

There are so many texts in Sanatana Dharma that reveal the depth and vastness of true spiritual knowledge and explain the nature of the world. But the minds of young people may not accept these texts in their original form. We should be able to express these scriptural teachings to the youth in a language they can understand, according to the times. This is the responsibility of the older generation. However this education should not merely be intellectual. When explaining spirituality to the youth, we also need to invoke the heart. The older generation should employ the approach of dialogue[12]. When approaching young people, we shouldn't try to demonstrate our own knowledge and erudition. We should become

---

[12] Saṁvāda.

one with them, understand their hearts and engage them in discussions. We should patiently and lovingly listen to their questions and criticism. We should approach them with compassion. Only such an approach will create a real change within them. Above all, we should set examples that will inspire them.

What is the relevance of spirituality? An ignorant person with no goal in life is, for all purposes, asleep. In fact, he is not an individual, but a crowd. Such people cannot make decisions because, just like a crowd, they have so many conflicting opinions. When one aspect of the mind creates something, another aspect strikes it down. All the efforts of such people are in vain. Not having any clear sense of direction, they just keep wandering through life. It is like tying a horse to each of the four sides of a vehicle and placing the reins in the hands of a sleeping driver. People like this have no scope for progress. Such are the lives of those without spiritual understanding. They think, *"I'm reaching my goal... I'm reaching my goal...,"* but in reality their lives are not moving forward. Finally, they collapse in exhaustion. Our minds are currently flowing outwards towards countless external objects. We should reorient them and discover the infinite strength that lies within. In fact, being a mere individual is not enough; we need to be a conscious individual. This is the purpose of spirituality. This knowledge should be passed on to the youth.

In today's world many people believe that the ability to interpret the spiritual truths however one pleases indicates one's calibre as a teacher of spirituality. Inability to do this is considered weakness. The spiritual truths should never be interpreted as we please. They should be transmitted in such a way that they aid in the development of both the individual and society. That is why those entrusted to pass on this knowledge should be mature, possess a mind capable of discriminative thinking[13] and have an expansive heart. Only then will

---

[13] *Viveka buddhi*—a mind that has attained the wisdom and subtlety to clearly differentiate between not only *dharma* and *adharma* [righteousness and unrighteousness] but, ultimately, the eternal and ephemeral.

goodness and nobility arise in those who receive the knowledge from them.

Today's youth are not satisfied with mere words. Modern information technology has allowed them access to so much more knowledge than the previous generation had. Today, dissemination of information is not a difficult task. Merely preaching does not create a dialogue. Not only will it fail to attract the youth, it won't attract anyone. Any change created through such lecturing is fleeting at best. We should explain to the youth what real dialogue is. This is the responsibility of the older generation. All of Swami Vivekananda's words were dialogues, as they were heartfelt and flowed forth from a perfect understanding of the intellectual and emotional level of the people to whom he was speaking. This is the source of the power behind his words. This is why even today his words continue to transform people.

Discussions are constantly taking place between the leaders of different religions and cultures, but we should re-examine whether the methodology and language employed in these discussions are truly adequate. Today, many of us are able to provide logical and intellectually satisfying interpretations, but we are forgetting to impart the beauty of the heart along with our logic. Meetings should not be a mere confluence of people; they should be a confluence of hearts.

Problems arise when we say, "My religion alone is good; yours is bad." This is like saying, "My mother is perfect; yours is a whore!" Only when we hold discussions with the understanding that each person sees his outlook as perfect will we be able to effectively communicate with others.

True religious leaders love and worship the whole creation, seeing it as a manifestation of divine consciousness. They see the unity behind the diversity. However, today, many religious leaders misinterpret the words and experiences of the ancient seers and prophets simply to exploit weak-minded people.

Religion and spirituality are keys meant to open our hearts, enabling us to view everyone with compassion. However our selfishness has blinded us. As a result, our minds have lost their power of discriminative thinking and our vision has become distorted. This is only serving to create more darkness. Due to our lack of discrimination, the very keys meant to open our hearts are locking them shut.

Once, four men were travelling by boat to attend a religious conference when they were caught in a storm and had to take shelter on a deserted island. It was a bitter-cold night. The temperature had fallen almost to freezing. Each traveller carried a matchbox and a small bundle of firewood in his pack, but each one thought that he was the only one with firewood and matches.

The first man thought, "Judging from the medallion around that man's neck, I would say he is from some other religion. If I start a fire, he will also benefit from its warmth. Why should I use my wood to warm him?"

The second man thought, "That person is from the country that has always fought against us. I wouldn't dream of using my wood to make him comfortable!"

The third man looked at one of the others and thought, "I know this guy. He belongs to a sect that always creates problems in my religion. I'm not going to use up my wood for his sake!"

The last man thought, "This guy has a different skin colour than mine, and I hate that! There's no way I'm going to use my wood for him!"

In the end, not one of them was willing to use his wood to warm the others, and so, by morning, they all froze to death. In reality, their cause of death was not the external cold. They died because of their frozen hearts. We are becoming like these men. We quarrel in the name of religion, caste, nation and skin colour, without showing any compassion towards our fellow beings.

Modern society is like a person suffering from an intense fever. As the fever soars, the patient says senseless things. Pointing at a chair on the floor, he may ask, "Why is that chair flying around?" How can we possibly answer? Most of us live like this. It is easy to wake a person who is sleeping, but it is impossible to wake someone pretending to be sleep.

The youth are attracted to Swami Vivekananda's words not merely because he spoke the language of logic and the intellect, but also due to his sincerity. At the World's Parliament of Religions in Chicago in 1893, when he began his speech with the words "Sisters and brothers of America!" the entire hall exploded with excitement and joy. Why? Because those words were so sincere and heartfelt. If there is sincerity in our words, they will definitely inspire and empower others. This in turn will motivate them to engage in selfless actions.

The foundation of all positive change is true education. True education is the secret *mantra* to obtain success in life. Such education is the solution to all problems. As Swami Vivekananda said, "What is education? Is it book-learning? No. Is it diverse knowledge? Not even that. The training by which the current and expression of will are brought under control and become fruitful is called education."

Currently, modern education only has one goal: worldly success. "Success" has become the mantra of our youth. "Whatever path you choose in life, you must succeed!" This is the motto of the modern educational system. Our education system has been reduced to a tool for obtaining material success. But will such success last? Will it help our children obtain love and respect from society? Will it provide them the strength needed to stand firm during the trials and tribulations of life? It may bring them some temporary gains, but eventually they will collapse.

Not only do we need to understand just how hollow, artificial and shallow this modern concept of success is, we also need to appreciate the meaning and import of true success in all its fullness. Regarding success, Swami Vivekananda said, "[The purpose of youth] is *atma-vikasa* [self-unfoldment]. It is *atma-nirmana* [self-development]. Please try to understand the correct implication of the term successful life. When you talk of success with reference to life, it does not merely mean succeeding in everything that you undertake.... The essence of true success is what you make of yourself. It is the conduct of life that you develop, it is the character that you cultivate and it is the type of person you become."

Those who attack their enemies with swords and guns are not the only soldiers. Anyone who strives to reach the goal of life is, in a way, a soldier. A *kshatriya*[14] is one who fights battles. Where? In every field of life. Whether it is in the field of art, politics, business, spirituality or education, we need to be able to invoke the qualities of *sattva*, *rajas* and *tamas* properly[15]. We need the mental faculties and vigour to focus all of our attention on the goal of life and move forward. To prevent selfishness, we need the light of goodness in our heart. We also need the ability to express this goodness. The motivation behind all of our

---

[14] One who belongs to the warrior caste in Hinduism's four-caste system.

[15] According to Hindu scriptures, the root materials of the universe, which include the human mind, are threefold: *sattva guna*, *rajoguna* and *tamoguna*. In this context, they represent the forces of sustenance, creation and destruction, respectively.

actions should be the holistic growth of society and the welfare of humanity. The growth of everyone includes our own growth as well. This is true growth. For this understanding to become firmly rooted in our mind, we need discrimination.

What the youth of today lack is proper discrimination. Merely by disseminating information, we cannot awaken discrimination in others. One can only develop discrimination after first developing faith in the power behind the cosmos—the power beyond our mind and intellect. We should eliminate the egoistic notion that our life will become fruitful through human effort alone. We should bow down. Only then will the power supporting the cosmos flow into us.

If we ask a guitarist or a singer where his music comes from, he will probably say, "From my heart." But if we surgically open his heart, will we find any music there? If he says that the music comes from his fingertips or his throat, would music be found if we searched those places? Then from where does music arise? It

Cultivating Strength & Vitality

arises from a place beyond the body and mind. This place is the abode of pure consciousness—God. The younger generation should strive to understand and respect this power. The modern education system does not give importance to cultivating this type of understanding. Youth should be made aware of the importance of love, selfless service, humility and the necessity of repaying society for its contribution to their success. Whether one is a householder, a CEO or even a political leader, the first thing we need to know is ourselves. This is true strength. We need to know and accept our own faults, shortcomings and limitations, and then try to overcome them. This is when a true leader is born.

True leaders are those who can lead others to the path of *dharma*[16] with self-confidence, sincerity and self-awareness. Today's youth will become tomorrow's leaders; therefore they should understand the source of true strength. Only when they develop a good heart and are

---

[16] A code of righteous conduct that takes into account the harmony of the world, society and the individual.

able to perform actions without any expectation will they begin to attract and influence the hearts of others.

Meditation and spirituality are inseparable aspects of life. A meditative mind and spiritual thinking are essential if we want clarity and subtlety in our thoughts and actions. To see spirituality and life as separate is sheer ignorance. Just as food and sleep are necessary for the body, spiritual thinking is necessary for a healthy mind. But how do we view meditation and spirituality today?

Once, two friends met along the roadside. The first man asked the other how he was doing.

"Fine, thanks," said the second man.

The first then asked, "How's your son? Did he get a job yet?"

"Oh, not yet, but he started meditating."

"Meditation? What's that?"

The second man replied, "Uh, I'm not quite sure, but I heard it's better than doing nothing."

Cultivating Strength & Vitality

Like this, many people think that spirituality is for those who have nothing better to do.

Spirituality is the core of Indian culture. If we imbibe our culture properly, we will find that it contains solutions to all of our problems as individuals and as a society. That is why Swami Vivekananda constantly extolled the youth to develop a heartfelt bond with their country and its culture. At the same time, they need to develop an independent intellect and open mind. They should find the courage to accept the good and reject the bad wherever they may find it. It is because Swami Vivekananda had these qualities that he was able to take pride in his Indian heritage and at the same time cultivate within himself the Western qualities of progressive thinking and dynamic action.

Vedanta is the foundation of India's all-embracing vision with regards to religion. It sees all religions as paths to the same goal. Swami Vivekananda prophesized that no matter how much modern science develops, the truths of Vedanta will stand firm, overcome any challenges and ultimately become a universal worldview.

Diversity is the nature of God's creation. This universe is too complex to be explained by any single religion or philosophy. If we want peace, contentment and progress, we should try our best to make the world understand the path of harmonious integration. In fact this harmonious integration is the very spirit of the all-embracing Sanatana Dharma.[17]

Amma sees the whole world as a flower. Each petal represents a nation. If one petal is infested with pests, it will affect the other petals as well. The beauty of the whole flower suffers. It is the responsibility of each and every one of us to protect and nurture this flower. Therefore all the nations of the world should advance together, hand in hand, sharing and adopting each others' worthy contributions and examples. When Amma says this, a picture of the roads in the West comes to Amma's mind. When Amma travels abroad and sees

---

[17] In its expansive vision, Sanatana Dharma contains many different views of the universe within its pliable framework.

the paved roads, cleanliness, discipline and order there, she wishes it were like that in India as well. If our roads were better, countless accidents could be avoided. If we cultivated the same cleanliness standards, prevention of epidemics and other diseases would be much easier. If we had the same work ethic, India's growth and development would flourish faster. Similarly, Western countries can imbibe India's worthy contributions—especially its spiritual wisdom.

There is one fact each Indian citizen should remember: our heritage is incomparable. What sheds light on the present is the impressions we've created within us through our past thoughts and actions. We should adopt the good from other countries while remaining firmly rooted in love for our own country and spiritual culture. When Sri Rama[18] reached the border of the kingdom of Ayodhya on his way to the forest, he gathered up a handful of soil

---

[18] In the Indian epic *Rāmāyaṇa*, Lord Rama, an incarnation of God, is exiled from his kingdom for 14 years.

and said, "Our birth mother and motherland are even greater than heaven itself."

After his first tour of the United States, when Swami Vivekananda reached Chennai, it is said that he rolled in the sand and proclaimed through tears, "Even after visiting so many countries, I've never found a mother like mine." When he stayed in a five-star hotel, instead of sleeping on its fancy bed, he lay down on the bare floor and shed tears, remembering India's poor and starving. Such love and respect for our country and culture should be the example for all of us, especially our youth. We should remember, "Our birth mother's rice gruel is tastier than our stepmother's sweet pudding."[19]

At a time when materialism and its stress on indulgence were gnawing away at the treasure of Indian culture, Swami Vivekananda arose with a pot of *amritam*[20] he had drawn

---

[19] The implied meaning is that the traditional cultural values of one's home country are ultimately more nourishing and satisfying than luxuries and pleasures gained abroad.

[20] In India's legends, the demigods and demons were both seeking *amṛtaṁ*—an ambrosial nectar that bestows immortality.

from the *rishi parampara*[21]. This is why Vivekananda was able to accomplish so much in such a short period of time, both in India and throughout the world. His words are capable of providing humanity the strength and self-confidence to face Himalayan obstacles, to swim across rivers of tears and deserts of hardship. He accepted sorrow and suffering as the greatest teachers. His life became a *deepa stambam* [a grand sacred lamp] of optimism to a people who were drowning in hopelessness. Before his birth, sannyasa meant detachment[22] from the problems of the world. Swami Vivekananda added to that intense detachment a focus on service based on the sweetness of love and the fragrance of worship.

Before concluding, Amma would like to share some extra ideas with her children:

1. It is not wrong for each person to believe his

Here, Amma uses the word to indicate the spiritual teachings of India, which lead to Self-realization as well as to a harmonious and prosperous society.

[21] The lineage of sages through which India's spiritual wisdom has been passed down since time immemorial.

[22] *Vairāgya*.

faith is right. However we should give others the freedom to their beliefs as well. When we force our religious beliefs upon others, religions born of love become cause for bloodshed. We should not allow religions that were intended as songs of peace to create disharmony and violence.

2. Before the British educational system, India's educational system was based on the *gurukula*[23] tradition. At that time, education was not a mere brain-to-brain transfer of worldly knowledge, but also a heart-to-heart transfer of spiritual culture. Knowledge and awareness of dharma are the two sides of the coin of education. From birth itself, parents would chant the name of God in the ears of their children. In this way, children would grow up chanting God's name. Later, they would be sent by their parents to a gurukula, where they would live the life of a *brahmachari*[24] and

---

[23] Literally, 'the guru's family.'
[24] A student—the first of the four stages of traditional Hindu life.

learn all the scriptures[25] from their guru. They would learn what life is, how to live and how to respond to the world. As a result, children matured into adults capable of discriminative thinking. They were lion-hearted and willing to dedicate their entire lives for the sake of truth. This was imbibed as part of their education. Modern society has to revive this by creating a system of education rooted in values and spiritual awareness.

3. Having an institution of sannyasis that served society was Buddha's idea, and Swami Vivekananda adopted that according to the needs of his time. One hundred years ago, he declared that *daridra narayana puja*—worshipping God in the form of the poor—was the need of the times. This remains true today. When the plague spread through Kolkata, he served the diseased with the same devotion with which he had served his guru, whom he believed to be an *avatara* [incarnation] of

---

[25] In the *gurukulas*, the children were taught both *parāvidya* and *aparāvidya*– spiritual wisdom and material sciences. Both are considered *śāstras*—scriptures.

God. He was even ready to sell Belur Math[26] if needed. The truth that everything we see in creation is the Creator himself was not mere intellectual knowledge for Swami Vivekananda. It was a continuous flow of energy that touched his heart and made his hands serve without rest.

4. Each of our fingerprints, faces and pairs of eyes are unique. Anything made from the same mould—whether it is a needle, a shoe or a doll—will be identical. However, in God's creation, no two blades of grass, no two flower petals, are the same. What then to say of human beings? God has sent each person to earth with a special hidden ability. Each of our births has a purpose that only we can fulfil. Discovering that special power within us is the purpose of our life. That is when life becomes meaningful—a joyous communion. True education helps us succeed in this. Swami Vivekananda clearly said that we need education that will

---

[26] Located near Kolkata, Belur Math is the headquarters of the ashram started by Swami Vivekananda and the other direct disciples of Sri Ramakrishna Paramahamsa.

help us to develop not only our intellect but our heart as well. A society in which everyone was identical would be mechanical and dead. The beauty of life is found in the sharing of diversity.

5. There is infinite power within each one of us. Today 90 percent of people do not realize this. We are born in sorrow, grow in sorrow and die in sorrow. We need the guidance of a Self-realized guru in order to discover the God-given talents within us, of which we are currently completely unaware. That a Swami Vivekananda emerged from the communion of Sri Ramakrishna and Narendra[27] is due to the glory of the guru alone.

6. We should teach our children basic religious tenets and values as part of their education. At the same time, it is crucial that we make them aware of the redeeming qualities of all religions, without giving importance to their differences. This is the only way to maintain mutual love and respect in modern society,

---

[27] The name of Swami Vivekananda before he took *sannyasa*

where religious diversity is an ever-increasing reality. Furthermore, the values imparted in our educational system should help instil hope and optimism in the face of any current difficulties the children may be facing in their lives. Swami Vivekananda's universal vision and powerful words make his writings and speeches perfect teachings for school children.

7. The curse upon our society is ignorance regarding our traditions and the basic spiritual principles. This needs to change. Amma has visited so many countries around the world and personally met so many people there. All of them—including the indigenous people of Australia, Africa and America—take pride in their heritage and traditions. But here in India many among us neither have understanding nor pride. In fact some of us even ridicule our culture. Only if we first lay a strong foundation can we hope to erect a tall building. Similarly, only if we have knowledge and pride in our forefathers and heritage can we create a radiant present and future. First we need to create the proper environment. This requires that we pay

special attention to the starving and illiterate. For this, we need to go into society and act. Swami Vivekananda also stressed the importance of educating women and allowing them to take their proper place in society. In short, we need to be prepared to adjust our attitude with the changing times, cultivate a mind that is ready to act, and then move forward along the path laid before us by Swami Vivekananda. May this institution be able to spread the life and message of Swami Vivekananda throughout the world and implement the plan of action initiated by him. Amma prays that this institution becomes a blessing to the whole world and that all the efforts of Amma's children bear fruit.

||oṁ lokāḥ samasthāḥ sukhino bhavantu||

May all the beings of all the worlds be happy.

Book Catalog
By Author

Sri Mata Amritanandamayi Devi
108 Quotes On Faith
108 Quotes On Love
Compassion, The Only Way To Peace: Paris Speech
Cultivating Strength And Vitality
Living In Harmony
May Peace And Happiness Prevail: Barcelona Speech
May Your Hearts Blossom: Chicago Speech
Practice Spiritual Values And Save The World: Delhi Speech
The Awakening Of Universal Motherhood: Geneva Speech
The Eternal Truth
The Infinite Potential Of Women: Jaipur Speech
Understanding And Collaboration Between Religions
Unity Is Peace: Interfaith Speech

Swami Amritaswarupananda Puri
Ammachi: A Biography
Awaken Children, Volumes 1-9
From Amma's Heart
Mother Of Sweet Bliss
The Color Of Rainbow

Swami Jnanamritananda Puri
Eternal Wisdom, Volumes 1-2

Swami Paramatmananda Puri
On The Road To Freedom Volumes 1-2
Talks, Volumes 1-6

Swami Purnamritananda Puri
Unforgettable Memories

Swami Ramakrishnananda Puri
Eye Of Wisdom
Racing Along The Razor's Edge
Secret Of Inner Peace
The Blessed Life
The Timeless Path
Ultimate Success

Swamini Krishnamrita Prana
Love Is The Answer
Sacred Journey
The Fragrance Of Pure Love
Torrential Love

M.A. Center Publications
1,000 Names Commentary
Archana Book (Large)
Archana Book (Small)
Being With Amma
Bhagavad Gita
Bhajanamritam, Volumes 1-6
Embracing The World
For My Children
Immortal Light
Lead Us To Purity
Lead Us To The Light
Man And Nature
My First Darshan
Puja: The Process Of Ritualistic Worship
Sri Lalitha Trishati Stotram

Amma's Websites

AMRITAPURI—Amma's Home Page
Teachings, Activities, Ashram Life, eServices, Yatra, Blogs and News
http://www.amritapuri.org

AMMA (Mata Amritanandamayi)
About Amma, Meeting Amma, Global Charities, Groups and Activities and Teachings
http://www.amma.org

EMBRACING THE WORLD®
Basic Needs, Emergencies, Environment, Research and News
http://www.embracingtheworld.org

AMRITA UNIVERSITY
About, Admissions, Campuses, Academics, Research, Global and News
http://www.amrita.edu

THE AMMA SHOP—Embracing the World® Books & Gifts Shop
Blog, Books, Complete Body, Home & Gifts, Jewelry, Music and Worship
http://www.theammashop.org

IAM—Integrated Amrita Meditation Technique®
Meditation Taught Free of Charge to the Public, Students, Prisoners and Military
http://www.amma.org/groups/north-america/projects/iam-meditation-classes

AMRITA PUJA
Types and Benefits of Pujas, Brahmasthanam Temple, Astrology Readings, Ordering Pujas
http://www.amritapuja.org

GREENFRIENDS
Growing Plants, Building Sustainable Environments, Education and Community Building
http://www.amma.org/groups/north-america/projects/green-friends

FACEBOOK
This is the Official Facebook Page to Connect with Amma
https://www.facebook.com/MataAmritanandamayi

DONATION PAGE
Please Help Support Amma's Charities Here:
http://www.amma.org/donations